My First Book of
AMERICAN FOLK SONGS

25 Favorite Pieces in Easy Piano Arrangements

Bergerac

With Illustrations by
Thea Kliros

DOVER PUBLICATIONS, INC.
New York

Bibliographical Note

My First Book of American Folk Songs: 25 Favorite Pieces in Easy Piano Arrangements is a new work, first published by Dover Publications, Inc., in 1995.

International Standard Book Number: 0-486-28885-4

Manufactured in the United States of America
Dover Publications, Inc., 31 East 2nd Street, Mineola, N.Y. 11501

Contents

(arranged in their approximate order of difficulty)

For Nicole

A FOLK SONG is like a window into the past. Because it was written such a long time ago, it tells us how people felt about things back then. Sometimes the words describe the special look of someone the song writer dearly loved. Sometimes the song is about love of country and the pride of being part of a hard-working, freedom-loving young nation. Some folk songs are deeply religious, and in some the tune and words are just full of fun and nonsense, running over with high spirits.

Here are different eras of the great American past, and different places where those long-gone families and friends gathered for all sorts of reasons: to ride the prairie, to fight a war, to dance and play, or just to have a good time.

We thank all of those unknown poets and musicians for the kind gift of words and music they left behind for us.

Bergerac
Summer 1995

Black Is the Color
of My True Love's Hair

Appalachian Folk Song

Yankee Doodle Dandy

Marching Song of the Revolutionary War

In a marching tempo

Fath - er'n I went down to camp a - long with Cap - tain Good - ing, There we saw the men and boys as thick as has - ty pud - ding.

2

3

The Gift to Be Simple

Traditional Shaker Tune

In a moderate walking tempo

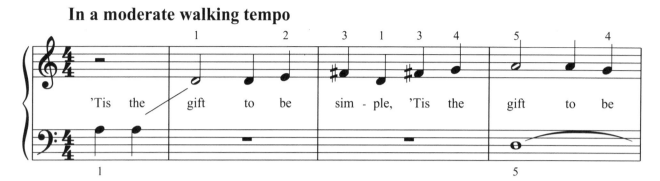

'Tis the gift to be sim - ple, 'Tis the gift to be

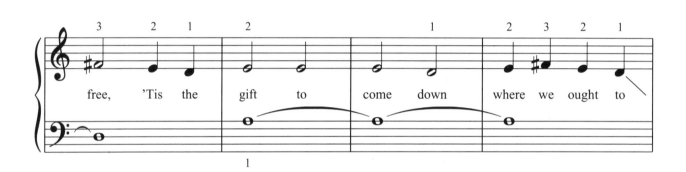

free, 'Tis the gift to come down where we ought to

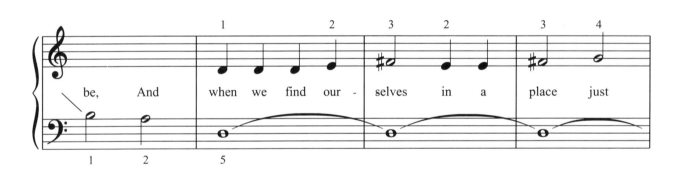

be, And when we find our - selves in a place just

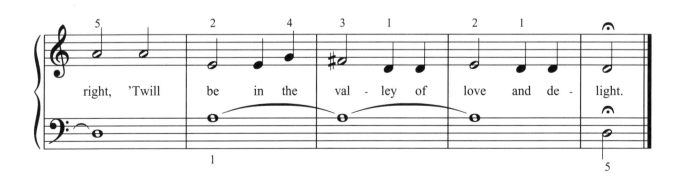

right, 'Twill be in the val - ley of love and de - light.

Aura Lea

Traditional "folk" tune based on the original song
by William Fosdick & George Poulton (1861)

Tenderly, but not too slow

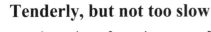

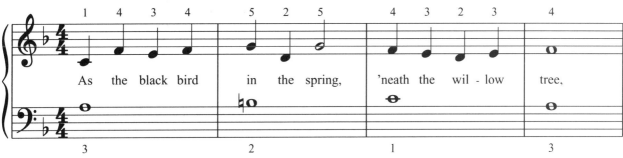

As the black bird in the spring, 'neath the wil - low tree,

Sat and piped I heard him sing, sing of Au - ra Lea.

Au - ra Lea, Au - ra Lea, maid of gold - en hair,

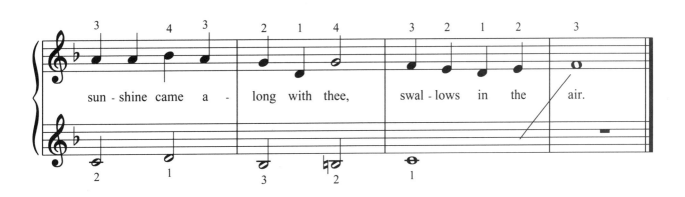

sun - shine came a - long with thee, swal - lows in the air.

5

Pop Goes the Weasel!

Children's Singing Game

At a lively pace

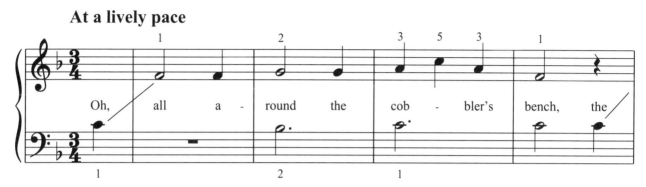

Oh, all a - round the cob - bler's bench, the

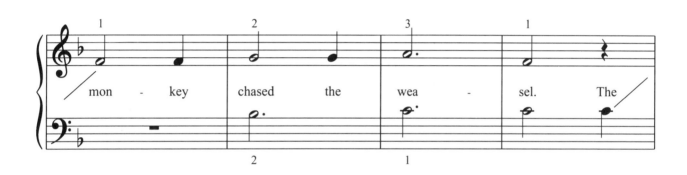

mon - key chased the wea - sel. The

mon - key thought 'twas all in fun,

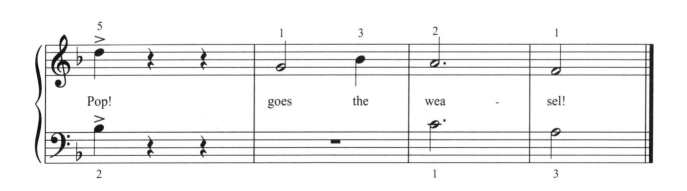

Pop! goes the wea - sel!

Amazing Grace

(Two-hand version in G major)

Spiritual

Flowing

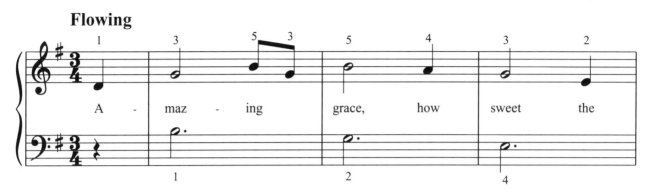

A - maz - ing grace, how sweet the

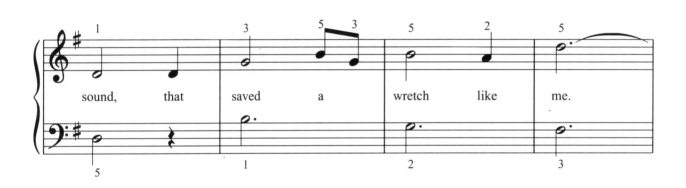

sound, that saved a wretch like me.

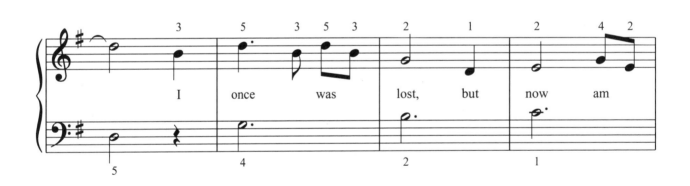

I once was lost, but now am

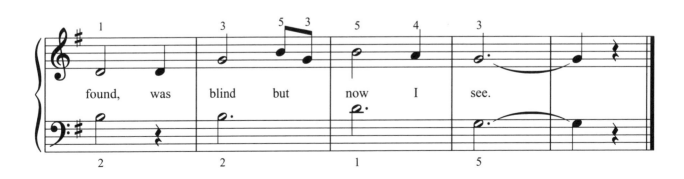

found, was blind but now I see.

Amazing Grace

(Right-hand version in G-flat major)

Spiritual

This time the right hand plays alone,
but only on the BLACK keys.

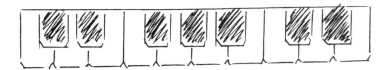

Flowing

A - maz - ing grace, how sweet the

sound, that saved a wretch like

me. I once was

lost, but now am found, was

blind but now I see.

Billy Boy

Folk Song of the Southern Mountaineers

Briskly (in 2)

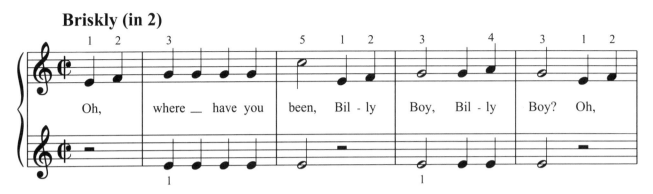

(Take your time!)

(Briskly again)

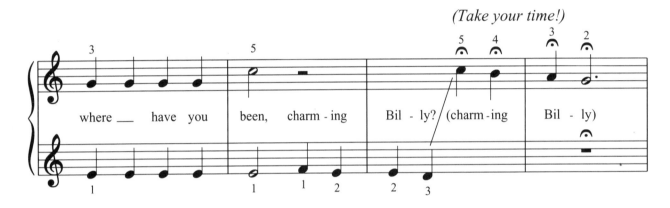

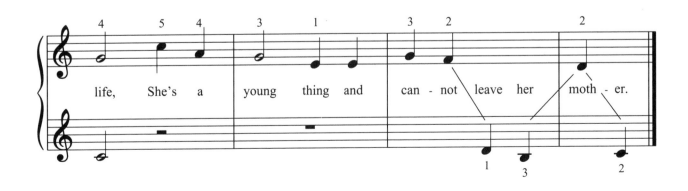

Buffalo Gals

A Western Square Dance

A lively, foot-tapping dance

Sweet Betsy from Pike

Traditional Wagoneers' Song

A gentle, lilting waltz

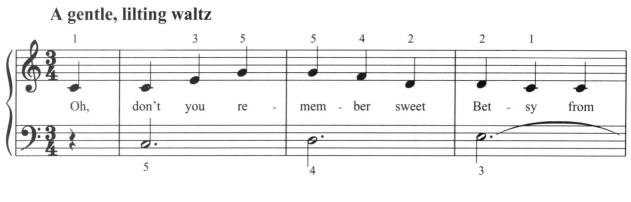

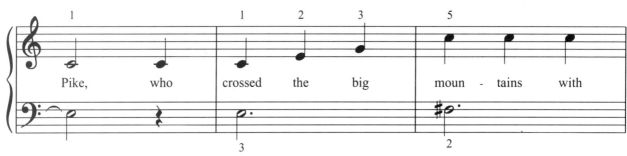

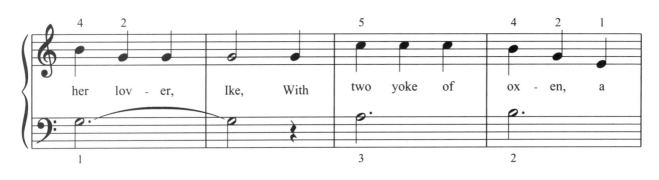

large yel - low   dog,   and a   tall Shang - hai

roost - er an'   one spot - ted   hog,   Sing - ing

"Too - ra - li,   oo - ra - li,   oo - ra - li - ay."

Thanksgiving Prayer

(We Gather Together)

Song of the Early Colonies

Skip to My Lou

"Play-Party" Dance of the Early Settlers

Lightly, not too fast

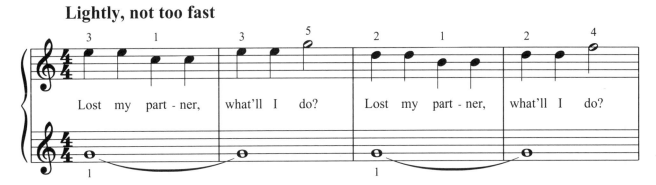

Lost my part - ner, what'll I do? Lost my part - ner, what'll I do?

Lost my part - ner, what'll I do? Skip to my lou, my dar - ling.

I got another one, skip, skip, skip! I got another one, skip, skip, skip!

I got another one, skip, skip, skip! Skip to my lou, my dar - ling.

Blow the Man Down!

American Sea Chantey

Swinging to and fro, with a good beat

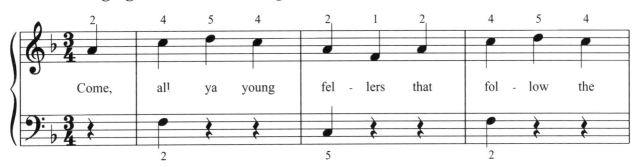

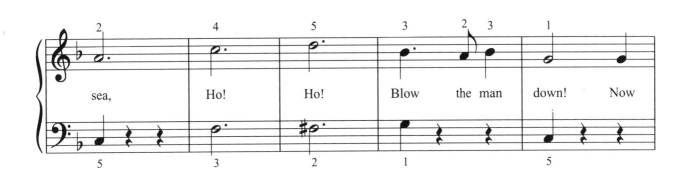

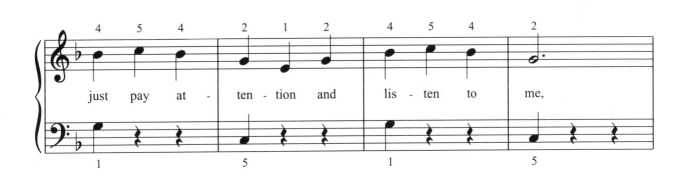

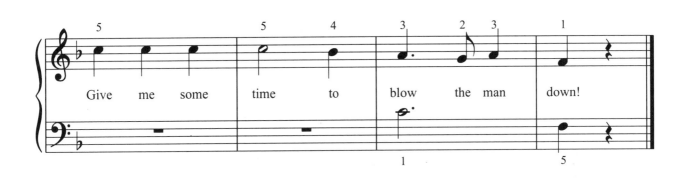

17

I've Been Working on the Railroad

Traditional American Work Song

With spirit and good humor

I've been work - ing on the rail - road

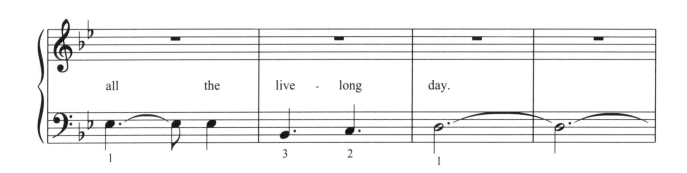

all the live - long day.

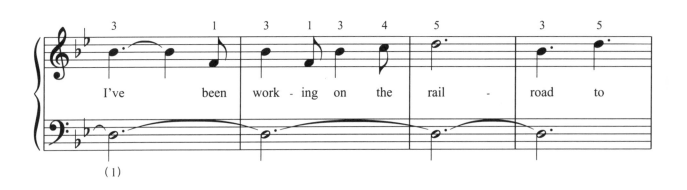

I've been work - ing on the rail - road to

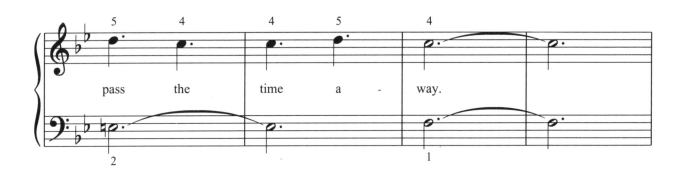

pass the time a - way.

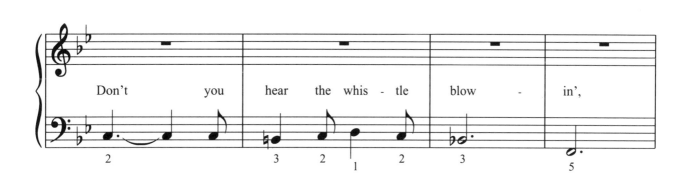

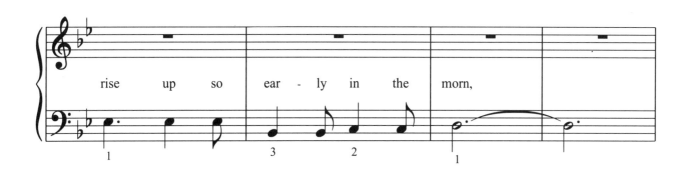

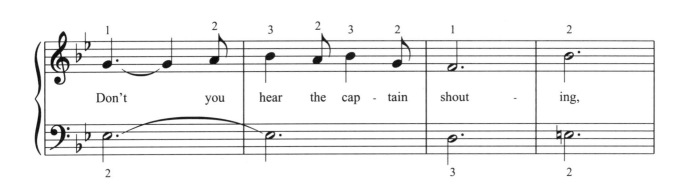

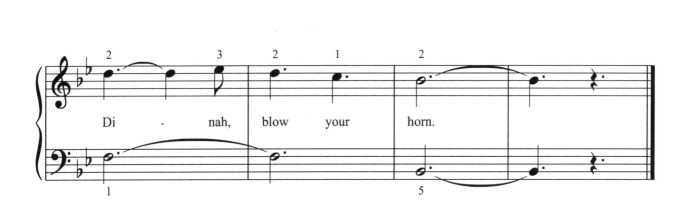

Blue-Tail Fly

(Jimmy Crack Corn)

Old Minstrel Tune

Take your time

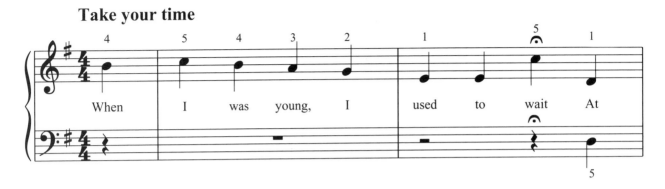

When I was young, I used to wait At

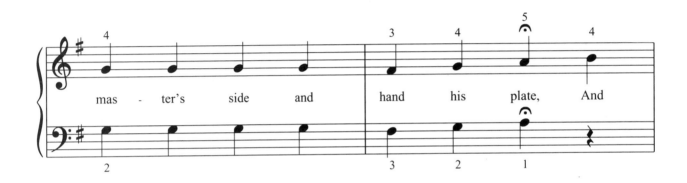

mas-ter's side and hand his plate, And

pass the bot-tle when he got dry, And

gradually quicker and brighter

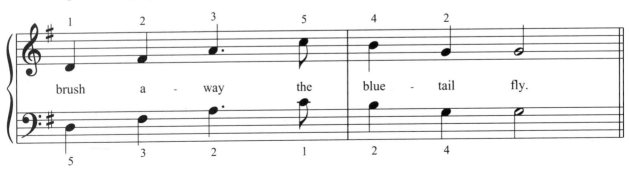

brush a-way the blue-tail fly.

Fast and funny

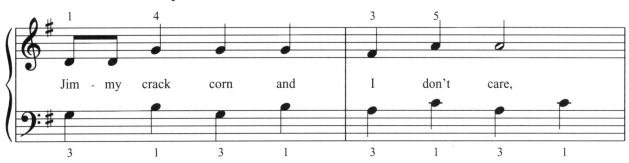

Jim - my crack corn and I don't care,

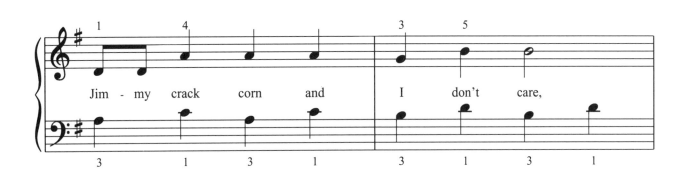

Jim - my crack corn and I don't care,

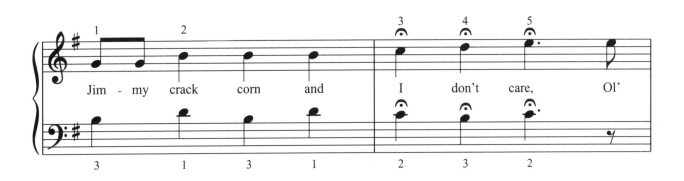

Jim - my crack corn and I don't care, Ol'

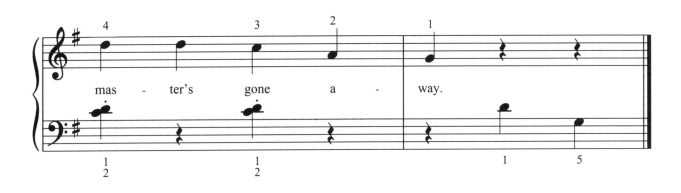

mas - ter's gone a - way.

The Farmer in the Dell

Children's Playing Song

Gaily (in 2)

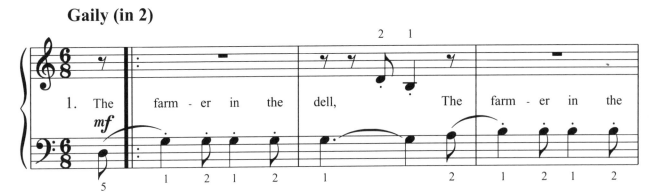

1. The farmer in the dell, The farm-er in the

dell, Heigh ho! the der - ry - o! The

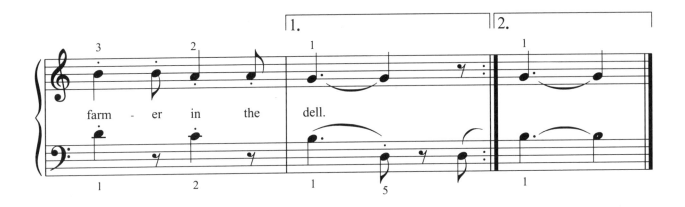

farm - er in the dell.

2. The farmer takes the wife,
   The farmer takes the wife,
   Heigh ho! the derry-o!
   The farmer takes the wife.

   (etc.)

The wife takes the child . . .
The child takes the nurse . . .
The nurse takes the dog . . .
The dog takes the cat . . .
The cat takes the rat . . .
The rat takes the cheese . . .
The cheese stands alone.

Turkey in the Straw

Early American Fiddle Tune

With a light-hearted bounce

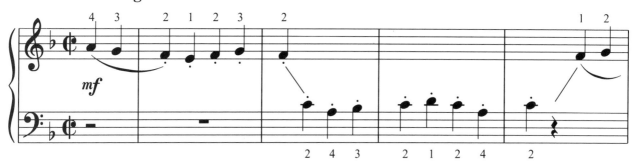

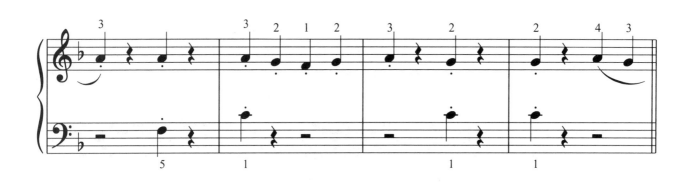

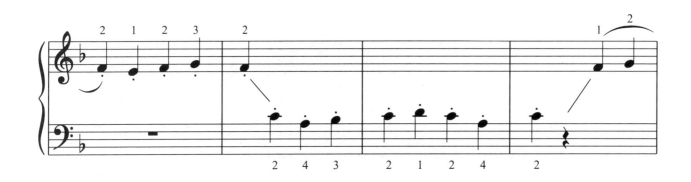

Deep River

Spiritual

In a quiet mood

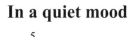

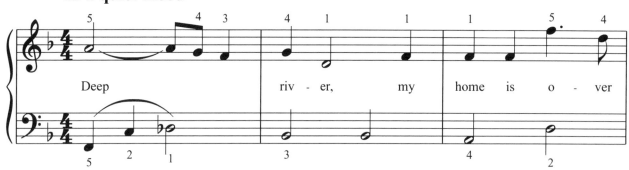

Deep   riv - er,   my   home is o - ver

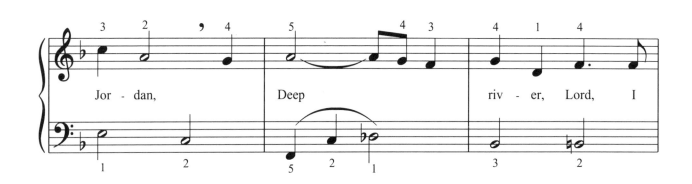

Jor - dan,   Deep   riv - er,   Lord,   I

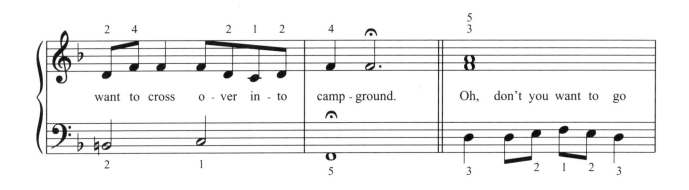

want to cross o - ver in - to   camp - ground.   Oh,   don't you want to go

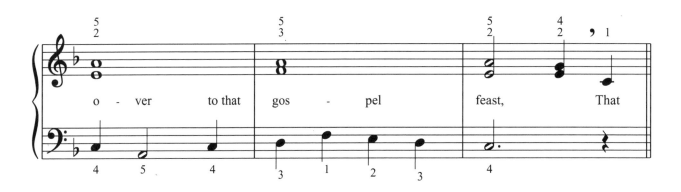

o - ver   to that   gos   -   pel   feast,   That

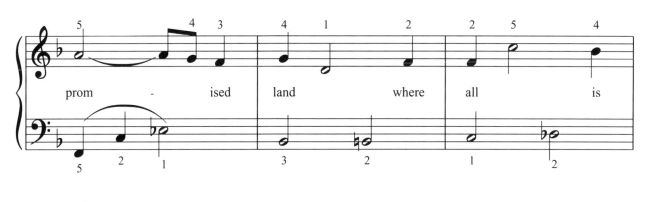

prom - ised land where all is

rit.   *a tempo*

peace. Oh, deep riv - er, my

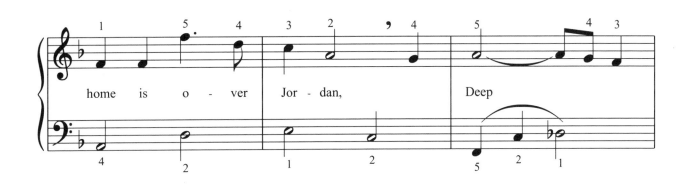

home is o - ver Jor - dan, Deep

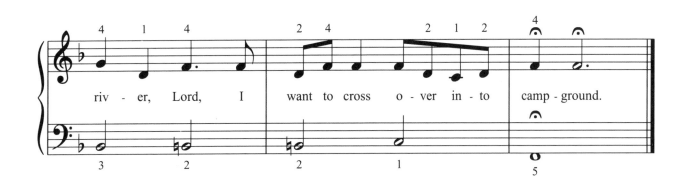

riv - er, Lord, I want to cross o - ver in - to camp - ground.

Down by the Riverside

Congregational Song

join hands with ev - 'ry - one, Down by the

riv - er - side, and stu - dy war no

more.

29

The Yellow Rose of Texas

Confederate Marching Song

INTRODUCTION

Slow and easy

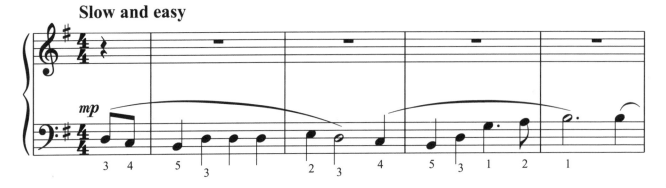

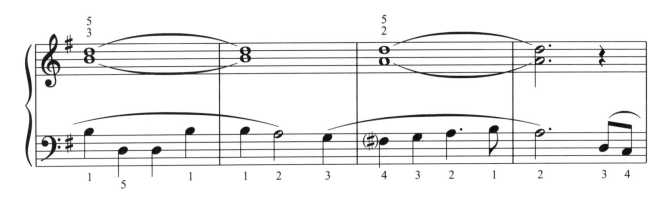

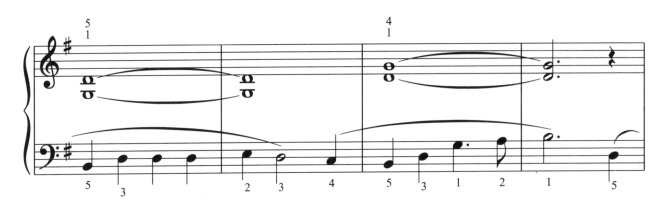

Fast and snappy

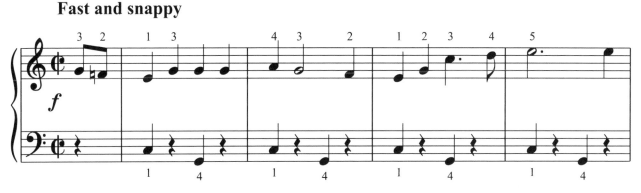

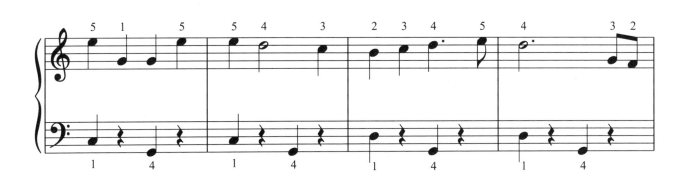

(etc.)

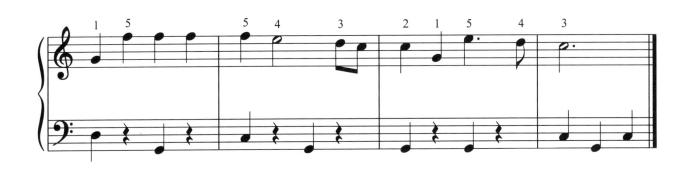

31

Short'nin' Bread

Song of the American South

Full of life and sparkle

(*p*, 2nd time)

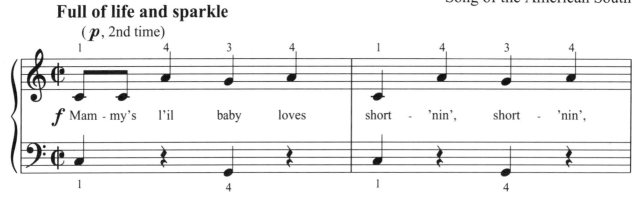

Mam - my's l'il baby loves short - 'nin', short - 'nin',

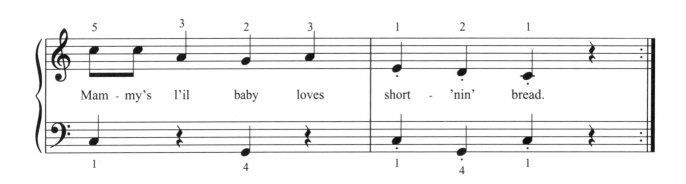

Mam - my's l'il baby loves short - 'nin' bread.

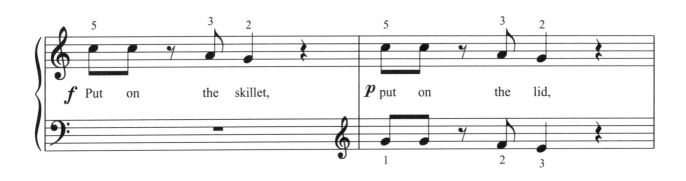

Put on the skillet, put on the lid,

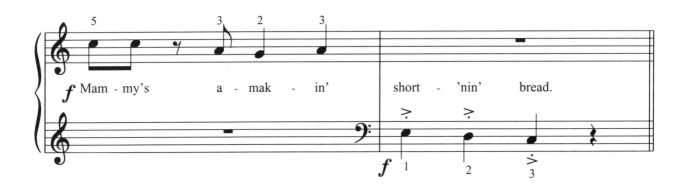

Mam - my's a - mak - in' short - 'nin' bread.

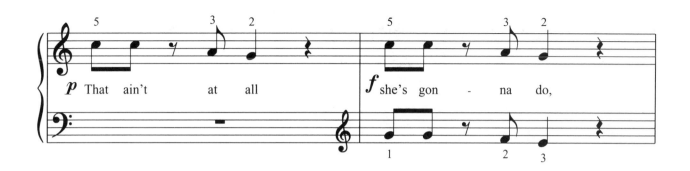

That ain't at all she's gon - na do,

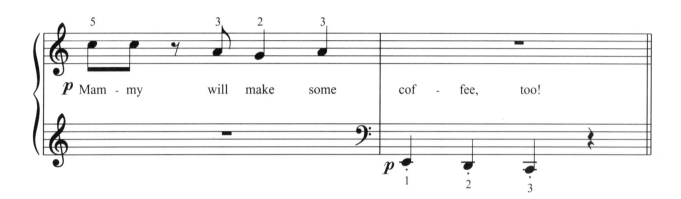

Mam - my will make some cof - fee, too!

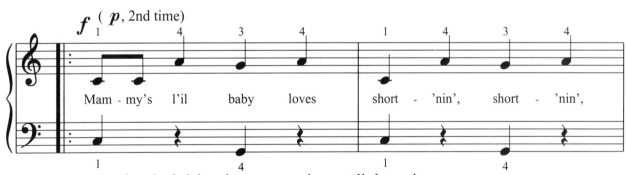

Mam - my's l'il baby loves short - 'nin', short - 'nin',

Or play the left hand one octave lower till the end.

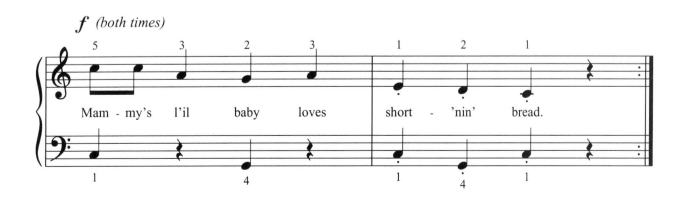

Mam - my's l'il baby loves short - 'nin' bread.

Polly-Wolly-Doodle

Early Minstrel Song

Light and lively

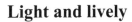

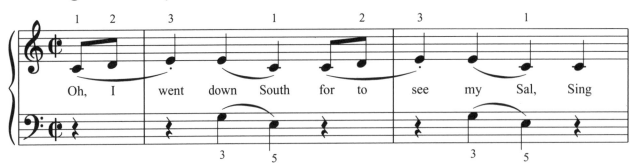

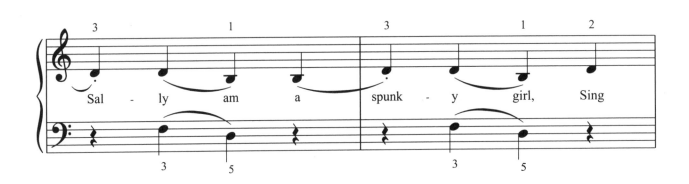

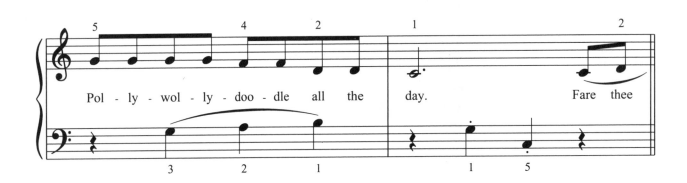

Go Down, Moses

(Let My People Go)

Freedom Song of the American Negro

Slowly, telling a story

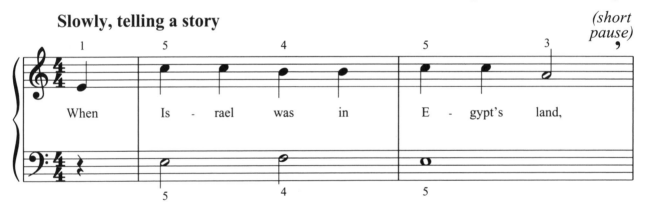

When Is - rael was in E - gypt's land,

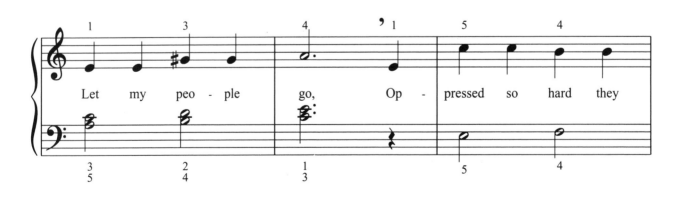

Let my peo - ple go, Op - pressed so hard they

Maryland, My Maryland!

Civil War Song

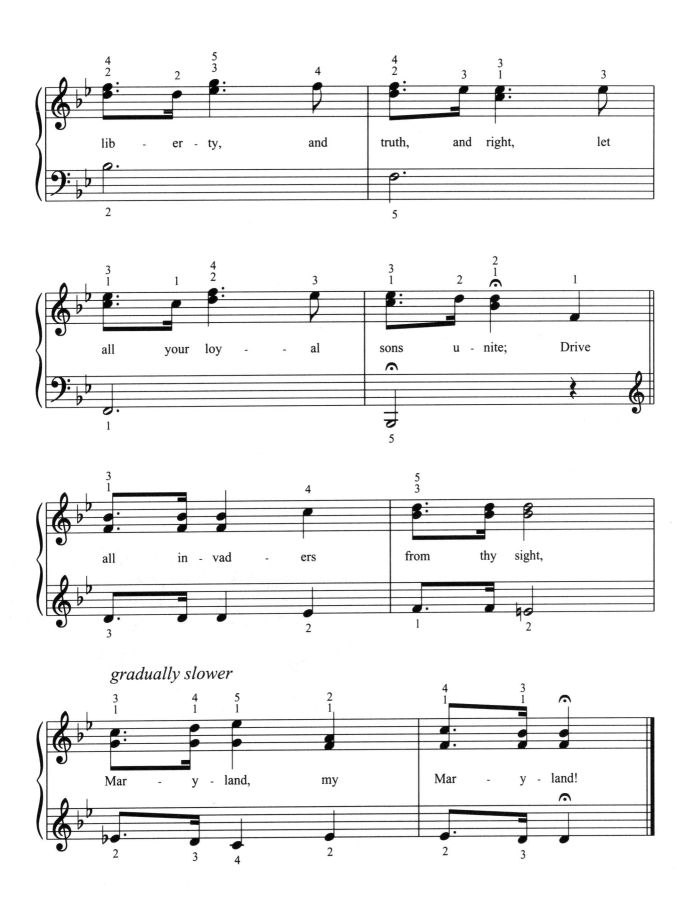

gradually slower

As We Go 'Round the Mulberry Bush

Colonial Children's Play Song

This is the way we wash our clothes,
All of a Monday morning.

This is the way we iron our clothes,
All of a Tuesday morning.

This is the way we scrub our floor,
All of a Wednesday morning.

This is the way we mend our clothes,
All of a Thursday morning.

This is the way we sweep the house,
All of a Friday morning.

This is the way we bake our bread,
All of a Saturday morning.

This is the way we go to church,
All of a Sunday morning.

The Old Chisholm Trail

Cowboy's Story-Song

Play the BLACK KEYS ONLY.

(Remember that a "flatted" note stays flatted within the same bar.)

Start slowly, then get faster and faster

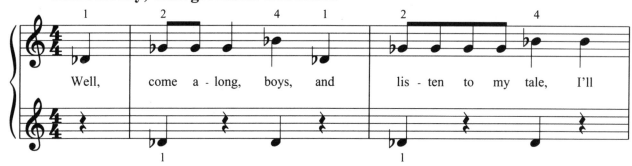

Well, come a-long, boys, and lis-ten to my tale, I'll

tell you all my trou-bles on the Old Chis-holm Trail, Come a-

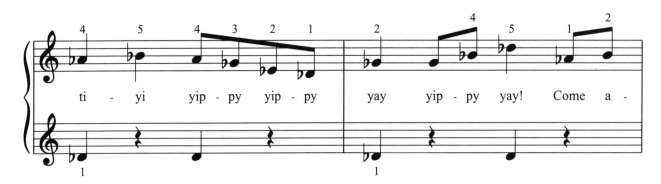

ti - yi yip-py yip-py yay yip-py yay! Come a-

(Repeat as you like)

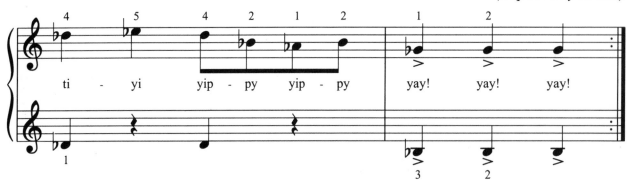

ti - yi yip-py yip-py yay! yay! yay!

42